Dingoes

by Mary Meinking

Consultant:
Blaire Van Valkenburgh
Professor
UCLA Department of Ecology and Evolutionary Biology

BEARPORT
PUBLISHING

New York, New York

Credits

Cover and Title Page, © Hemera/Thinkstock; 4–5, 6–7, © Susan Flashman/iStockphoto;
8–9, © J & C Sohns/PicturePress/Alamy; 10–11, © iStockphoto/Thinkstock; 12–13,
© Minden Pictures/SuperStock; 14–15, © Susan Flashman/Shutterstock; 16, © Jordan
Tan/Shutterstock; 16–17, © Bartussek/ARCO/naturepl.com; 18–19, © Minden Pictures/
SuperStock; 20–21, © iStockphoto/Thinkstock; 22T, © Susan Flashman/Shutterstock; 22B,
23T, © iStockphoto/Thinkstock; 23B, © CraigRJD/iStockphoto.

Publisher: Kenn Goin
Senior Editor: Joyce Tavolacci
Creative Director: Spencer Brinker
Design: Becky Daum
Photo Researcher: Arnold Ringstad

Library of Congress Cataloging-in-Publication Data

Meinking, Mary.
  Dingoes / by Mary Meinking ; consultant: Blaire Van Valkenburgh.
     p. cm. — (Wild canine pups)
  Audience: 6–9.
  Includes bibliographical references and index.
  ISBN 978-1-61772-930-0 (library binding) — ISBN 1-61772-930-2 (library binding)
  1. Dingo—Infancy—Juvenile literature. I. Van Valkenburgh, Blaire. II. Title.
  QL795.D5M45 2014
  599.77′2—dc23
                              2013008956

For more information, write to Bearport Publishing Company, Inc., 45 West 21st Street,
Suite 3B, New York, New York 10010. Printed in the United States of America.

10 9 8 7 6 5 4 3 2 1

🐾 Contents 🐾

Meet dingo pups

Three-week-old dingo pups snuggle in their **den**.

Their bellies are full after drinking their mother's milk.

Now, they are ready to sleep.

What is a dingo?

Dingoes are wild dogs that have yellow or brown fur.

They are about as big as a medium-sized pet dog.

Although dingoes look like pet dogs, they act more like wolves.

Adult dingo size

For example, they howl like wolves and rarely bark.

Where do dingoes live?

Dingoes are found in Australia and Asia.

They live in deserts, forests, and grassy areas.

Asia

Pacific Ocean

Indian Ocean

Australia

N
W • E
S

☐ Where dingoes live

Dingoes live in family groups called packs.

Each pack has its own **territory** where it lives and raises pups.

dingo pack

Starting a family

When male and female dingoes are ready to have pups, they **mate**.

After two months, the female prepares to give birth.

She finds a den in a cave or in a hollow tree.

Inside the den, she has four to ten pups.

11

Newborn pups

Dingo pups are born with their eyes closed.

After two weeks, their eyes open.

They can now see their brothers and sisters!

For the first three weeks, the pups never leave the den.

Time to go outside

When the pups are almost one month old, they explore outside their den.

They sniff plants, climb rocks, and play.

When they are two months old, they leave the den for good.

They are now ready to join the pack.

However, the pups are still too young to hunt.

Eating meat

Adults in the pack hunt for meat to feed the pups.

Dingoes eat rabbits, birds, lizards, and even kangaroos.

With the meat in their bellies, the adults return to the pups.

Then they spit up the food for the hungry babies to eat.

kangaroo

17

Hunting

When the pups are four months old, they begin to hunt.

They can catch small animals, such as mice, on their own.

However, the pups work with adults to attack kangaroos and big lizards.

lizard

Growing up

By the time the dingoes are one year old, their parents have new pups.

The year-old dingoes help raise these pups.

They guard the tiny babies from **predators**, such as crocodiles.

The young adults are learning how to take care of a family.

Soon, they will become parents themselves!

21

Glossary

den (DEN) a home where wild animals can rest, hide from enemies, and have babies

mate (MAYT) to come together to have young

predators (PRED-uh-turz) animals that hunt and eat other animals

territory (TER-uh-*tor*-ee) an area of land where animals live and hunt

Index

Read more

Koler-Matznick, Janice. *The Dingo (Library of Wolves and Wild Dogs).* New York: PowerKids Press (2002).

Sirota, Lyn A. *Dingoes (Pebble Plus: Australian Animals).* Mankato, MN: Capstone Press (2010).

Learn more online

To learn more about dingoes, visit
www.bearportpublishing.com/WildCaninePups

About the author

Mary Meinking is the author of 23 nonfiction children's books. She works as a graphic designer during the day. In her spare time, Mary enjoys traveling, photography, crafts, and writing for children. She lives with her family on a lake in northwest Iowa, where she watches wildlife year-round.